Peppern
Crean

GW01340207

Written by Barrie Wade and Maggie Moore
Illustrated by Bethan Matthews

Collins Educational
An Imprint of HarperCollins*Publishers*

Pete, Kulbir and Anna were at Kim's house. It was a Secret Club Saturday. It was also a wet Saturday. They couldn't go into the garden, they couldn't play ball and they couldn't go to the park.

"What are we going to do?" asked Pete.

Anna said, "I don't know. How about a jigsaw? Monopoly? Snakes and Ladders?"

Kulbir said, "No, I'm tired of those. Can we play on your computer, Kim?"

"No," replied Kim. "Dad's working on it this morning."

Kim's mum came into the room.

"Have you thought of anything to do yet?" she asked.

"No, Mum," said Kim. "We're trying to think of something different."

Kim's mum said, "How about cooking? I thought you could make some peppermint creams for Mother's Day. They're easy to make, so you can get on with them yourselves."

"That's a good idea," said Anna. "Thanks, Mrs Luk."

"It'll be fun," said Pete.

In the kitchen Mrs Luk put an old cloth and a small bread board on the table. She found the recipe. Then she opened cupboards and took out bottles, packets and mixing bowls and put them on the table.

"Here you are," she said. "You don't need a saucepan or the oven, so you can't hurt yourselves. Check that you have all the ingredients before you start. When you need to use the knife, Kim, your dad will help. He'll be at his computer. I'm going to work this morning. Now don't forget to wash your hands first."

After they had washed their hands, Kim said, "Let's read the recipe. My mum always reads the recipe before she starts to cook."

Peppermint Creams

Ingredients

Peppermint essence
Chocolate strands
Green food colouring
Block of fondant

1 Knead the fondant until soft.

2 Add a few drops of colouring and knead the fondant until it is an even colour.

3 Add a few drops of peppermint essence and knead it in.

4 Make the fondant into a long roll.

5 Cut it into segments. This should make about twenty peppermint creams.

6 Shape the segments into round pieces like large buttons.

7 Place the chocolate strands on a large plate.

8 Dip each peppermint cream into water and roll it in the chocolate strands.

9 Put each peppermint cream into a paper case when it is dry.

"Right," said Pete. "Let's check the ingredients. Peppermint essence." He picked up a small bottle.

"What's next?" Kim asked him.

"Green food colouring," read Pete.

Anna found it and said, "Here it is."

Kim read the next ingredient. "Chocolate strands," she said.

"Here's the packet," Kulbir said.

Kim went on. “And what’s this?” she asked. “Block of…”

Pete looked at the recipe with Kim. Then he picked up the only packet left.

“This must be it,” said Pete, holding the packet. “But what does it say? Fon… dant. It says fondant.”

Kulbir said, “Never heard of it.”

“Right,” said Pete. “We’ve got everything. What do we do first?”

"What's this word," asked Anna, looking at the first instruction. "K... n... e... a... d."

Kim looked over her shoulder. "You don't say the 'k'," she said.

"Oh," said Anna. "I can read it now."

> *Number one. Knead the fondant until soft.*

"What does knead mean?"

"I'll ask Dad," said Kim.

"It means press it and pull it over and over with your hands," she said when she came back.

Kulbir said quickly, "I'll do the kneading."

He took the fondant out of the packet and began to knead it on the bread board. He pressed and pulled for a long time.

"That'll do," said Pete, "you're dropping it all over the floor."

"Okay," said Kulbir. "Let's do the next bit. I'll read it."

> *Number two. Add a few drops of colouring and knead the fondant again until it is an even colour.*

"Oh, good. More kneading," said Kulbir.

Anna said, "My turn next."

While Anna was kneading, Kim picked up the bottle of green colouring and took off the top.

"Careful," said Pete. "It says a few drops."

"Okay, okay," said Kim. She held the bottle over the fondant.

Just then, Kulbir reached for the recipe and accidentally knocked Kim's elbow.

Green colouring gushed over the fondant, over the board and over the cloth. The four of them went quiet.

"Oh, no," whispered Kim.

They all stared in horror as the green colour spread over the cloth.

"Oh dear, oh dear," said Mr Luk from the doorway. "I thought something was wrong when everything went quiet."

"Oh, Dad, I'm sorry," said Kim. "I didn't mean it."

"It wasn't her fault," said Anna, Pete and Kulbir together.

Kulbir said, "I bumped into her, Mr Luk."

"Never mind," said Kim's dad. "No use crying over spilt green food colouring. Anna, get that bowl. Pete, hold that fondant on the board and pour the colouring into the bowl. That's right. Now I'll put the cloth in to soak."

Mr Luk put a clean cloth and a clean board on the table. "Okay," he said. "Ready to start again? You'll have to knead all the green colouring in, all of it."

Everyone had a go until the fondant was an even green. So were everyone's hands.

"I've got a house full of Martians," said Mr Luk, and they all laughed. "What's next?"

Kulbir picked up the recipe and read on.

Number three. Add a few drops of peppermint essence and knead it in.

"Kim, only a few drops, please" said her dad.

Kim said, "Someone else can do that. I'll do the kneading this time."

Kulbir undid the bottle of essence and sniffed it. "Gosh! That's strong."

Kim said, "That's why you only need a few drops."

Kulbir took a teaspoon from a drawer and poured a few drops onto the spoon. Then he tipped it onto the fondant. Kim kneaded the fondant until the essence was mixed in.

"I'll read next," said Anna.

Number four. Make the fondant into a long roll.

"Here goes," she said. She rolled the fondant.

"Look at my roll," she said.

Kulbir said, "Here's the next bit."

Number five. Cut it into segments. This should make about twenty peppermint creams.

"What's segments?" asked Anna.

"It's just pieces, like segments of an orange," explained Kim.

Mr Luk made a small knife mark where the segments should be cut. He did this carefully so that each of the cooks got five pieces.

Then he handed Kulbir the knife. “Be careful,” he said.

Kulbir cut the twenty segments. Anna, Kim, Pete and Kulbir each had five pieces.

"I'll read the next bit," said Pete.

Number six. Shape the segments into round pieces like large buttons.

Anna, Kim, Pete and Kulbir shaped their pieces into buttons and put them in a row in front of them.

"Next stage," said Kim, taking a turn at reading the recipe.

Number seven. Place the chocolate strands on a large plate.

"There's no plate," said Anna.

"I'll get one for you," said Mr Luk, reaching into the cupboard.

Anna got the chocolate ready and then read on.

Number eight. Dip each peppermint cream into water and roll it in the chocolate strands.

"We'll need a bowl of water for that," said Kulbir. They dipped their peppermint buttons into the water and rolled them in the chocolate strands.

"Next bit's the last," said Pete.

Number nine. Put each peppermint cream into a paper case when it is dry.

“We’ve got to wait until they’re dry,” said Pete. “What shall we do while we’re waiting?”

Kim said, “It’s stopped raining. We could go outside.”

Her dad said, “I’ve got a better idea.”

“What’s that?” asked Kim.

Mr Luk smiled. “Sweeping up, washing up and drying up,” he said. “Look at this kitchen.”

They all looked around. Bits of white and green fondant were on the floor and on the table. There were two very sticky boards. Chocolate strands were all over the cloth. Then they looked at each other and began to laugh. Their hands were green and their mouths were brown.

"First wash your hands and faces and then tidy the kitchen," said Mr Luk. "Then the sweets should be dry."

"Can we try one as soon as they're dry?" asked Kulbir. "We've got to make sure they taste right, haven't we?"

"Yes," said the others together.

"Well, I suppose you can have just one each," said Mr Luk. "We'll keep it our secret."